facture

Raymond de Borja is the author of *they day daze*, and *as well, in our estrangement*.

ISBN: 978-1-915760-37-1

Cover designed by Aaron Kent

Edited and Typeset by Aaron Kent

Broken Sleep Books Ltd
Rhydwen
Talgarreg
Ceredigion
SA44 4HB

Broken Sleep Books Ltd
Fair View
St Georges Road
Cornwall
PL26 7YH

In conversation with cultural figures as varied as Agnes Martin, On Kawara, Walter Benjamin, Guy Debord and Eva Hesse, Raymond de Borja's *facture* exists snugly between the interstices of prose and poetry, rhetoric and lyric. 'I want our poem to have a face. It needs a way out of it' writes de Borja in 'What of Our Renewed Interest in Utopia' and the poetic face seen by this reader is one craggy with wonder, verve, and brass. This poetry is a broken machine fragmented into erudite perfection. *facture* desires to be nothing but itself, and de Borja's poems linger deep beyond the breadth of the page. You can't go home again, no, but luckily you don't want to.

— Jeff Alessandrelli, *Nothing of the Month Club*

de Borja's *facture* is both exacting in its articulations and impossible to cage into any single denotation. Here is the wilderness of language reinventing itself even as it is understood through the lineage of art making. This text lets us rebuild our attitude toward how fact can create a rapport with the fracture of all that we understand to be knowable. What most thrills me here is that there is, beyond intellectualism, a throughline of emotion that can draw us deeper into the intuitions of the artists and art practices de Borja brings to us.

— Rusty Morrison, *Beyond the Chainlink*

'Gesture means defective products haphazardly, daily, slipping past, forever, from our fingers,' writes Raymond de Borja in *facture*. Our hands find it hard to keep things, our hands cannot stop things from eluding us: de Borja engages with conditions of ephemerality and precarity in this book, which follows *they day daze* and *as well, in our estrangement*. De Borja responds to emergencies of the everyday through gestures of gathering: as in, citation; as in, to assemble—with vertiginous intelligence—references to, among others, Toru Takemitsu, Walter Benjamin, On Kawara, Kurt Schwitters, Gordon Matta-Clark, and Trisha Brown. From this assemblage, de Borja creates places, however temporary, to shore against loss: "citation as site, and *facture* as the material fact of joy." While *facture* can evoke, on the one hand, materials, it can also enact, on the other hand, gestures of putting materials together, which, in de Borja's case, means collage: 'then us placed side-by-side as if in lyric we.' More importantly, for de Borja, to collage is to construct communities by other means: 'a sociality which renders the unlikely union of [Agnes] Martin and Guy [Debord] in a sentence.' *facture*'s world—our world now—is fallen; by 'break[ing] things that are not broken, and fix[ing] things that are,' de Borja disputes these conditions. For de Borja, correspondences—resituated citations—index new prospects: *facture* is a book 'where various cities touch without tremor.'

— Vincenz Serrano, *Now is the New No*

Also by Raymond de Borja

they day daze   (HighChair, 2012)

as well, in our estrangement   (Aklat Ulagad, 2022)

Contents

facture

Raymond de Borja

Broken Sleep Books

So Facture is the Material Fact of Joy

It is the fifth of April 1976. As an alternative to concrete response, which can be violent, and to transcendent response, which can be detached, Agnes Martin speaks of an abstract response. "We are in the midst of reality," she says, "responding with joy."

It is the seventeenth of May 1961. For the *Research Group on Everyday Life*, Guy Debord clicks on his tape recorder which begins to deliver his prerecorded lecture.

But while everyone agrees on the being of reality, Debord needs to insist on the existence of everyday life, despite the sociologists.

Can we say that this altering of our experience of a lecture is responding with joy?

In Agnes Martin, the experience of joy is elusive because it is rare.

In Guy Debord, we find life that is structured by the scarcity of free time.

It is everyday life which gives reality and joy a palpability. A sociality which renders the unlikely union of Agnes and Guy in a sentence: We are in everyday life responding with joy — an experience that is scarce and rare.

This sentence requires a studio where we can wait, or where we can walk —

A willed reception, a radical waiting; we wait for falling blue;

Or we walk up a fire exit because the rusting on its rails appears like a cloud of burnt sienna, a radiating color field, then we find a satellite dish. We break away from our dérive with each the task of bringing back a microwave oven.

For elusiveness, attention.

For scarcity, choice and risk.

So Martin's *Gabriel* is attentively looking at the virtual from the actual, and seeing, for 78 minutes through the beach and the mountains, horizontal bands of color. While in Debord's *La Société du Spectacle*, it is montage after montage of text spliced to image that forms a spectacular whole.

We can trace a common thread of generosity running in these studios. When Agnes Martin speaks of joy, it is joy factured in everyday life.

An "awareness

of the profound richness and energy abandoned in everyday life inseparable"

from an "awareness
of the poverty of the dominant organization of this life."

So we quote Guy Debord.

But Agnes cautions us on the experience of others: we are "in reality at a standstill, because their experience is in the past."

Which is why we respond with the lyric,

and in choosing the lyric, live with a text long enough, attentively enough, to begin to imagine for it, more than this experience, a prosody, a text inscribed in present time.

This requires a studio, where we can cite and quote, that persists in the present. Citation as site, and facture as the material fact of joy.

Grids

to mark that we have located something which we cannot possess; that is not knowledge; we are happy.

Grids unquote.

For morning, for falling blue, for loving love

for earnestly pondering slight alterations of usual procedures

the everyday right here   How

is our life

We Write a Song for the Brand-new Equipment

A derrick inscribed in a factory inscribed in a body of water inscribed in a letter. Factories in the work of interpretation; a letter arises from circumstance, manufactures without interruption. Dear Jean, the interruption above our heads like a sun, which the devout sees dancing, which Apollinaire beheads. Trough, to crest, to hear things with the same astonishment. Echo in eye, resonant among, last Monday, in the warehouse of missing parts.

Excursus to Utopia

The science has touched upon what we jettisoned
away. A metal needle to steer the ship. Soft
calamity. Problems of association.
Into commerce against my will. The constant nothing
meeting danger. Its will announcing the weather.
Stringed nullities, future's echoes, bees attracted to work.

Then met in human terms, a chemical model
of reason, measured harm, accumulation of
tone. Motes suspended in a beam of the fiscal
spirit. Which nature mirrors. Point in pivot. Mise
en abyme. Pivot in point. In chemical terms,
this human model. The clocks expected. Spirit to work.

And perennially we. Like music overcome.
By a memory of numbers. An interval
minimum. Harmonized rest. Then the hymn is sung.
Then the rest harmonized — acoustical fieldwork.
Architecture rapt in the growing of flowers.
Sunrise held. In every phalanstery. From work to work.

Then the traces read questions concerning habits
of mind. Our post-industrial charm. The uses
of prophecy, any number of enticements.
If the operations of if interiorized
opera. The operative world distracted.
Its widened scope. A swallow flits by. On the way to work

And the reveries compiled. The management of
forests. By means of sound. A god or matter writ
till rote. Appeared anonymously in Lyon.
The passional events ending when. Whence, when sung.
Given consequence. A pure sentiment forms.
When gathered together. As if by chance. Meaning to work.

The True Picture of the Past Whizzes By

(Automaton)

The Greek inventor Ctesibius creates the first water-powered cuckoo clock in the Library of Alexandria; the sculptor Daedalus uses quicksilver to give his statues movement and voice; a bronze eagle, constructed by Hephaestus, feeds on Prometheus's liver.

Strings and mirrors, the illusion on the table, the illusion of a table, the partially material mouth.

There was once, we know, an automaton constructed in such a way that it could respond to every move by a chess player with a countermove that would ensure the winning of the game.

The results, different each night, are surprisingly human.

And beautiful not because infinitely deferred but because inconsistent in its logic of appearance.

(Lotze)

Zoe Leonard desires to take up her Rolleiflex and photograph "every single object in the world, every product of human manufacture."

We harmonize by omitting, our necessary fragments and gaps, and almost call it loving.

Our participation in this self-making (see for example, a comedy).

"It is one of the most noteworthy peculiarities of the human heart," writes Lotze, "that so much selfishness in individuals coexists with the general lack of envy which every present day feels toward its future."

Depreciation is planned obsolescence.

(L'Ordre)

A chronicler remembers the great and small, pictures that are our private language, texture that means we are touching speech.

Of course only a redeemed mankind is granted the fullness of its past — which is to say, only for a redeemed mankind has its past become citable in all its moments.

How else might we imagine a different social order were we to make speech out of our human condition?

Passionate believers — we go on anticipating the spirituality of technical labor.

"Who am I?" begins Breton's *Nadja.*

(Marx)

When asked about her marriage, Jenny von Westphalen was touted to have said, "Yes we were happy enough, but I wish dear Karl could have spent some time acquiring capital instead of writing about it."

We are at a point in our lives when currency speculation is more profitable than surplus labor; value creates value.

It said, "Phlogiston, caloric, corpuscle," words with no real referent, "the luminiferous aether."

They are alive in this struggle as confidence, courage, humor, cunning, and fortitude, and have effects that reach far back into the past.

It said: "Grab the book nearest you" — the third sentence of the fourth chapter describes your life.

(Point)

The past can be seized only as an image that flashes up at the moment of its recognizability, and is never seen again.

But viewed from another moment, a point is a line, and a line is a surface illuminating its surrounding space.

Which is to say, your presence is required.

For a moment, the previous scene's rubble floats over your worried face as if you were water.

The people of the future have the constant expression of hyperawareness — isn't cinema about someone, anyone going after an image?

(Receivers)

We take today's headline, something that unexpectedly appears, and the way things really are, then give their relationship a sound.

Everything (after crossing the boundary between the visible and the invisible, the living and the dead, buffer zones, phases of matter...) ends up in some sort of receiver.

It means appropriating a memory as it flashes up in a moment of danger.

The immediate past is in the present as a sideward glance; the present moment built out of many sideward glances.

Is the ear shaped like a receiver, or the receiver shaped liked an ear?

(Opera)

Barbarism from the Greek "barbaros" meaning foreign, related to the Sanskrit "barbaras" meaning stammering.

There is no document of culture which is not at the same time a document of barbarism.

She means to ask, "Are you also a foreigner?" but instead she says, "Are you also a stranger?"

Sight-reading parts that are meant to be song.

An empathetic listener sees you stammering with your hands.

(Amazement)

A Sunday with light rain, music for chase scenes, then music for murder.

An anecdote beginning: Documents take the place of dreams.

Two blocks away from the stock exchange, at the Bibliothèque Nationale, Georges Bataille, studying coins.

We are poised at the beginning of knowledge, our faces backlit with words.

This amazement is not the beginning of knowledge —

(Angel)

A baroque filter heightens our experience of daily life.

On the desk sounds come from nowhere, photographic evidence of angels, and photographs of sound.

The angel would like to stay, awaken the dead, and make whole what has been smashed.

In January 2012, the Eastman Kodak Company files for Chapter 11 bankruptcy protection.

For angels, read bankers; for aura, read filters.

(Cause)

Because in the end we end up with nothing in our hands but signs, with nothing in our signs, why —

Because a body in motion, why —, because a body at rest.

The themes which monastic discipline assigned to friars for meditation were designed to turn them away from the world and its affairs.

Because the full apparatus for recreating the scene: a real mountain, real people on vacation, why —

Because here is a woman with rose-colored sunglasses, who will have cause in the future to grieve, but doesn't know it yet.

(Fourier)

According to Fourier, cooperative labor would increase efficiency to such an extent that four moons would illuminate the sky at night, the polar ice caps would recede, seawater would no longer taste salty, and beasts of prey would do man's bidding.

And what of the evidential quality of the work?

Language dreams in form: the self-portrait of the working class: a sky-full of apertures.

Either we allow the plumbing and the wiring to show, or draw over it a veneer.

As a result, the currencies of twelve member-countries are replaced by the Euro.

(Garden)

We need history, but our need for it differs from that of the jaded idlers in the garden of knowledge.

In 1974, Gordon Matta-Clark procures a plot of land measuring one hundred by one square feet on Lafayette Street, New York.

Things omitted: a scholium on green, a garden in the marginalia.

Yet by some kind of error, we are here.

To have and to hold the premises herein granted unto the second party, the heirs or successors and assigns of the second party forever.

(Itself)

It was such a unique product but it needed on it a human face to make a connection.

Second, it was something boundless (in keeping with an infinite perfectibility of humanity).

It was John Berger's voice saying that whenever van Gogh painted a road, "the roadmakers" were present "in his imagination."

It was music.

Cinema's a constantly updating cloud.

(Thus)

Fashion has a nose for the topical, no matter where it stirs in the thickets of long ago.

Now something seen, something described; now, something referred to, something returning, in the form of a question.

Thus, when Condillac imagined his statue gaining one by one each of the five senses, he endowed it with first the sense of smell.

Then mannequins — their medium specificity.

Now it comes to us radical and decorative, a garage sale to spark commerce among our private selves.

(Action)

Frame where actions take their place, place under natural light, light's arrested quality.

Who witnesses sees only song.

Then us placed side-by-side as if in lyric we.

An eyewitness, who may have owed his insight to the rhyme, wrote as follows.

But the subject sees differently, attempts to sing of common air.

(Cannot)

For this notion defines the very present in which he himself is writing history.

We cannot figure out for instance whose memory it is.

Then lines approach the present each with its desirous pause.

The we which we are and cannot ever be there.

Eva Hesse writes Sol Lewitt, "You asked me to write, Sol, closeness and not knowing enough. Another's world. I cannot know your world."

(Method)

It involves words, the definitions of words, the definitions of the definitions of words, until a garden, before erasure, in the pause before naming, where the wheel, where the wheel is a cup, where the cup the inner ear, where the face a fact.

Thinking involves not only the movement of thoughts, but their arrest as well.

Trace recorded in its vanishing, a faint architecture.

The seeable caesurae: The paragraph's a tracking shot.

And then we find Proust withstanding sleep, sleepily writing sentences.

(Hour)

In tracing the emergence of the uniform, monetized hours of factory time, Edward Palmer Thompson begins with lines from Geoffrey Chaucer, where a rooster: "Wel sikerer was his crowyng in his logge/ Than is a clokke, or an abbey orlogge."

Or, as a kind of abbreviation, the present that we share.

On this scale, the history of civilized mankind would take up one-fifth of the last second of the last hour.

Where the hour of leisure is the hour of work?

"No" she says, "that's not it."

The Emergences, The Pause

The difficulty of narrating anything to you at all

This is we leaving the cinema

Feeling at the tipping point to fact

Mini-worlds will, as we are wont to hear, spin to a minimal music

Much of our afternoons filled with laughter and socialism

The emergences, the pause

Between this sentence and the next takes years

In between, a cryo-frozen brain is linked back to a body

Which at first feels the need to yawn

Cut to another yawn

Then another

Until dailiness is a mouth

The musical equivalent of

Then We Dream You Together

Arc to narrative arc subtends

You have the awe of someone who cannot remember

If the atmosphere imperceptible to actors
where a comma hangs
were we to pause in air

Where to change our way of speaking
is to change our lives

To wake and find our speeches in the air

Trope by frayed trope
an account of morning

You have the awe of someone who cannot forget

Trembling before the marvels of industry

Then we dream you together
trembling with excitement

You have the awe of someone

Else, devoured by ornament
we change our lives

To wake and find us sutured to a place
and by waking tug the atmosphere
with our skin

Arch to arch subtends

You have the awe of someone else

Scissioned from your skin

To wake and understand you need this in your life
so speak it lovingly

You have someone else's awe
so speak it, lovingly

Trope by trope
our frayed speech

Before the marvels of industry

To wake and understand you need this in your life
so want for it a prosody

Between the Making of This Move
and This Move

Then left to the quiet of gesture. The shoulders see to it that the arms see to it that the hands. The hands, the fingers. The fingers time, space, then intensity.

"And I don't know whether I can go back again to abstraction," says Trisha Brown after working on Claudio Monteverdi's *L'Orfeo*.

The Monteverdi, whose *chorus of spirits* makes Trisha pace around her studio, asking herself "what is a spirit, what is a spirit," makes her find a vocabulary of movement without

bone structure, that is smoke, intensity

draws forward the head
where the body, while, where the distance
between gesture and movement is a note

or a fullness of presence.

And the distance between gesture and writing is the sign
as the sign for itself.

Dear Jean, we are
lost in the repetition, a color,
or a phrase of movement

recalls to us *Écriture Rose* by Simon Hantaï —

which begins green,
begins black. Hegel: *In making its
inorganic nature organic*

to himself

and taking possession of it for himself. Looked at, however,

Ends in black. Maintains the missing.
And the quiet is the fold.

Where what is accomplished in writing
is the color rose.

It is after parting ways with surrealism that Simon Hantaï begins his work with folds, begins the search for "an unremarkable painting."

"The underpinning of my work is to create an architecture that is solid," says Trisha Brown "so the audience will know what the changes are."

In working with Bach's *The Musical Offering*, Trisha returns to the question "What is a theme?" takes a walk thinking "what is a theme, what is a theme."

It is fifteen years after withdrawing from the art scene that Simon begins work on *Travaux de lecture* as requested by his friend Jean-Luc

copying, re-copying, copying, re-copying Jean-Luc's and Jacques'

until an unreadable manuscript results on the stiffened and crumpled batiste.

Mailed to Jean-Luc as a gift in March 2000.

Word is where the work turns
is read as color is relation.

So the work
in the economy of the gift must be held in relation
may be word.

Silence whose rigor is a kind of sensuality
and whose sensuality is a line

Asked to put our arms around the work

The section of Trisha Brown's *Set and Reset* where she dances with
Eva Karczag and her gestural movements are mirrored by Eva's
balletic motion.

The shadow of the musculature on their backs
from the lighting design
of Robert Rauschenberg.

Dear Jean, we are chosen for how we sound. Dance means deixis as
a fullness in the present.

Before Simon Hantaï's silence, some shorter silences, and several
pliage works: *Etudes et blancs, Tabula* —

which Simon destroys, buries, and after his return from silence,
unearths, and makes into new work which he calls *Leftovers.*

There is a photograph of Trisha Brown performing *Watermotor*
(shot by Babette Mangolte) where she seems to be moving
simultaneously to her left and to her right.

"My father died in between the making of this move and this move," Trisha finds herself saying in a performance of *Accumulation with Talking Plus Watermotor*.

In lieu of a biography, Simon Hantaï includes in the catalogue of his 1976 retrospective a photograph of a large unfolded painting, and a grainy, black and white picture of his mother wearing a dark, creased, gridded tablier.

"And I don't know whether I can go back to abstraction again." Trisha Brown says after working on *L'Orfeo*.

What Felt Like the Onset of an Historical Emotion

Or a mind. Is the silent ligature between the glass, the ornamental grass, and an idea of enclosure. Should not saying anything structure an imagination — sublime render, place improbable grandeur, trial sublime.

Now You Are Faintly Beginning

In the opposite direction, a moment of surprise,
surroundings faintly heard

Pages missing, many dangers exist
complete with thunderbolts

But not violently, no, but in a gesture of a new beginning

And clearly, you are the woman in the plane crash at the beginning

We take the position of strangers at every beginning

In the opposite direction, complete with thunderbolts,
the clarity of dangers

But not violently, no, but in the direction of pages turning

And our surroundings are gestures faintly beginning

And our surroundings are gestures
faintly heard

Strangers at each violent beginning

The plane missing, the pages, the danger of clarity
complete with thunderbolts

Where moments of surprise are directions faintly heard

In the now you are faintly beginning

No, we have gone missing

Strange dangers, a plane turning complete with thunderbolts

In the direction of now's turning

Surroundings turn gestures into clear dangers

And violently, yes, as with new surroundings

The plane crash at the beginning,
now, is missing

Now, we have gone missing

A Dream of Anechoic Chambers

A great crack in the afternoon. Probably a
heart. I forget to say towards.
This century's exactitude. Collecting
signatures. Factories
for the duration of a war. An adaptation of.
Thence every masterpiece.
Then the long years of prosperity.

Apparently, evening. Our first reaction was.
To want to return. A passage cited. In the middle of.
In the middle of. A pamphlet her response became.
A scrutiny of miracles. The modernity
of her. Announces the weather.
The theater is only theater.
Then the long years of prosperity.

Around the time of analysis. Having long slumbered.
Textual forests where the accent falls. Alas, the
sadness of a bourgeois. Drones in place.
In exchange. And oddly 19th century.
Where work begins experience. A Sunday. A feeling
that sensuous specificity must be mythless. Or leisure.
Then the long years of prosperity.

Chord shifts stuck in the head. A past composed
purely of peripheral scenes. Flickers between
disrepair. A chapter on trauma.
Almost certainly upon us. Anterior to.
The development of sound. Sacred, signifying,
Returning syllables to the O of.
Then the long years of prosperity.

We say no and then. No wonder.
Out of a thicket of marvels, the regularity
of thickets. The physiology of an individual.
The physiology of a city. The typology
of acquiring a life.
A life is a worrisome limit.
Then the long years of prosperity.

Until the magic goes wrong. Insistent
ringing. One turns to the word
for rabbit. To the word
for hat. The claque breaks
into song. But the deeper explanation
for all of this is again. Those hidden doors.
Then the long years of prosperity.

Obscure sorrows. First the mark
then the market. In a dream of anechoic
chambers of commerce. In our voice
the words of strangers. A delay
in the vitreous scenes. A colon caught
in a sigh suspends the analogy.
Then the long years of prosperity.

To excise a piece of sound. Were
it flowers. At some distance
derricks. Dissolve in ambient chatter.
What you said. Just now
in the dense interleaving.
A face. Naming thus.
Then the long years of prosperity.

I forget the word for recognition. I forget
the spiraling downward motion of speech.
The perimeter of a wing. Motion
worked as thought, I forget muscle, gristle,
and bone. Absences and containments.
I forget whether rain, static, or perforations.
Then the long years of prosperity.

Clothe

I dreamt I fell asleep for a few minutes, exhausted

Screech unfolds in the must

Filigree seen from behind the fretwork

Is our tortured face, is our absent look
Was it "pine for me"

Composed differently the wound

And still confused with now and cotton

Cut first, then measure

Work

1

They produce it by
googling silicate.

Do you think
it would've shown?

Days come because it.
Bus noise, indent guess,
syndetic intense need
in constant receiving.

Meet them voice.
In the loop do it through his voice —

zoom, hoist, threaten, and describe.
We all fit this meet.

So this morning's Vincent swings easy,

sees auditions, does photography so vivid
this event will noise.

Did you take me sleep?
Didn't we do
incidence of you?

2

This intimacy due to production:
evening deviations, avoidance thunder.
I need to send the commission. Let Siri
do it. I need to institute a hunch.

Someone said to give it a month so I've been at it,

the dictation that it was
undid the message.

Soon,
you will ship it.

You will do a diptych on difference.

Spending time so good
between the big big white screen of Joseph Stalin
and some chic house of Shakespeare.

3

Weekends saw us on the hunt
for the sign like a shock
and the shock like more of the same

perfume knit to the site
the Meissen dogs hunt for.

4

Lists leak into the swishing space
an argument stuck between Alice and Blake.
The last link you liked,
liked by many since, is now a year.

But "you are dead" in the bulletin already.
We met there, remember? And had your ID signed
then voided, and oh,
that worried look on your face
cause you felt like it.

5

We were deep into the meeting
when appeared the gift of dormancy
with the lighting instruments
with the sleeping speech
when we asked for something else
you kept our focus on Alice
venting musicals in time

6

To some this is still
about you. There is that.

To others, about their ways,
there is much

that needs to be done.
We are about

to have an excellent month.

7

The quality of noon peaks,
spinning in the given. Houses
with 3D cabinets, oblique towns swiped
with slant beauty, light-eaten. We begin
in field's distributed song. Windows all
along. Variously responding shine.
Knotted solution.

8

The space we hastily made between the show
and its scholium.

In each district listed,
the volume decreased.

Day, we said,
what little forgetting.

9

And in our Siri voices say goodbye

to one phenomenal student of life

10

The new took. The evening

in display. The hour defaults to dust

in the basement union.

11

The machine speaks mostly
in captcha

of our default need for days,
for entire weeks.

For hours
we are lost in technique.

12

Then Mondays made for games
of seek and you shall find.
Stunned House. Sick Light.
We point at massive spondee signs.

13

The harsh light excepted
by design, replaced with cottoning
light. Trees thinking
side by side. Our rebooted scope
picks-up your tree-character's illumined
thought. Green then
yellow with the gloaming.

14

In noise we see the divine
infused with more
of the divine

"I hear you," says one technician
of the divine

Morning's material time
at our last snooze
awaits us.

15

Our long days
are studies
in hope-effects.
Even we
are moved
so we have
to decide

Orphic Data Lakes

The morning air enveloped precisely to mean *good
morning — the scene of the crime — today
slightly overcast.*

These are meant for us.
In our light-like separation, hear from ourselves
our static-curtained songs.

In Orphée, a radio unwraps from the netherworld *A glass
of water illuminates the world.*

Attention says the radio *Silence
goes faster backwards The bird
sings with five fingers...*

Which Cocteau first finds in a letter from Apollinaire.

Progress is air, all that is solid.

Of the Eiffel Tower, Apollinaire sees
a massive antenna.

Dear Jean,
pillars of salt infrastructure is code orphic data lakes.

I wish, today, I could tell you these
with the illocutionary force of fact.

World that is a world of rests.

We Have Altered the Ways in Which We Hear Music

Or haloed with words — The compositional meets the sensory — is how we are written — is where the phenomenal — self — whispers — is where error meets erratum — when the invention of noise — leaves — where I am made with — expectation — which the present open — reopens.

Where What We Feel and the Afternoon Are Topologically the Same

Construction, Walter Benjamin quotes Sigfried Giedion in Convolute K, *plays the role of the subconscious.* Bright moments between an instant and attention. We seek immediacy by hewing as close as possible to design. Gesture means defective products haphazardly, daily, slipping past, forever, from our fingers. But gesture is a dream, and dailiness the sheen about our dream objects, about our longue durée.

A House Collaged With Pitch Class Space

Daylight glosses the living room floors of M and Mme Leiseville at 27-29 rue Beaubourg.

Daylight at a doorless threshold, from several iterations of Les Halles, from the construction site of the Centre Pompidou.

Daylight at the rubble-edges of Gordon Matta-Clark's *Conical Intersect*.

Then daylight at the apex, collapses, of a person's cone of vision.

We expect the high-pitched ring that accompanies suddenly something bright

instead of silence annexed to shimmer, interior glow, found sounds, an audience pointing to the sun, and a critique of modern housing.

Cones of vision and funnels of hearing emanate from an audience, transform the light-holes into points of articulation.

Construction sounds enter our gardens.

Passersby with their wobbly cones and funnels escape analysis.

The "particular agony" that Toru Takemitsu finds "in the sound of the door someone closed" is our hearing in place of analysis.

We are when our geometric imagination meets social space, a schematic diagram of a house collaged with pitch class space.

The semi-circular incisions across floors, ceilings, and walls involve chisels, saws, hammers, and an extraordinary amount of sound.

"Gardens are constructions of space," says Takemitsu, "so really what I do is compose gardens with music."

Gardens with construction sounds strain toward the present.

Perhaps, a light-split wall is how composition intersects construction as the immaterial spatially arranging,

or a movement where the phrase sustained by an oboe continues to the shō.

The moments after his dream, where Toru begins to compose *A Flock Descends into a Pentagonal Garden*.

A shape that is a modulation, and not a modularity.

A morning, when we are, where construction is composition.

The shape that sound acquires from trusses, rubble, incision, this pastoral's dream content, our found ways of being, Dear Jean, the varied surfaces of our listenings, "a lyrical cutting through"

suffused with light, where dream and labor intersect.

The Given Is What Accident Refracts to a Gift

Set where various cities touch without tremor — the timbre of a tear — offered — in the fabric of — to a listening where — when straining for — there — when towards — disambiguation — an attentive ear — understands — that it cannot understand — the impulse towards — what we feel we mean — when saying here.

After Music

This very evening, Jean, they are ripping the square apart

As each idea forecloses an image of the world

Our now, this here, the instances of documentation

Light-eaten

Moth-eaten world

The music that description means interface becomes experience

White on white noise

Ambient form whose form is the intrusion of speech

In after-office sunrise, painted on noise

World on world

Your face discloses where light was

In Malevich, 1915, *Red Square* or the *Painterly Realism of a Peasant Woman in Two Dimensions*

Word on word remains

When describing color is to fix the I until the names unfasten

Malevich, for whom *the town has lost its colors*, for whom *the significant thing is feeling*

Dear Jean, the riot is our figure and our ground

If light were separable from gesture, the interpretation of the real
is our documents set to music

But we're not

Kafkaesque

Begins in Greenwich, England
Mildews as a verb

Refrains, i.e.
Never, never, never, never, never

And returns to an absolute ear
with its every no

An even longer line
at the end of every line

We were there implied in each erasure
like a hankering for

Whose you is mine?

But the time we dealt with
was human time

A Fold

Laughter latticed light
a line that is white and softens
into a flourish of lace

then muted   switches to a ringing

in the ears   then muted

A light that makes us doubt even the music that we hear

The one that is playing now

"Sublime" passes through your lips

Laughter shatters texture shatters laughter

Dear Jean, this is set in a dream full of talkative people and textile

Its edges are linen and doubt

A party that takes place
at a blast furnace photographed
by Hilla and Bernd Becher

where the dreamlight
of heavy industry
reacquaints us to a face

We Requested for Relaxing Forest Sounds

We are lost in the exact study of appearance. The particular wavers between: authenticity and appropriation, a quaver, one's tying of a knot, oh please disemplot, one, someone, anyone, point by point from nature, in light rain, in sound, motes accidental, birds' precise unknowability, the present volume increases as it recedes.

What of Our Renewed Interest in Utopia

Dear Jean, you say that my poems lack people, so I people them. Then you ask to see their faces. Exposition is when appearance unfolds in language. The people walk past, speaking with enviable clarity. What is exposed by their gaits? Agamben says *there is a face whenever something reaches the level of exposition and tries to grasp its own being exposed, whenever a being that appears sinks in that appearance and has to find a way out of it.* I want our poem to have a face. It needs a way out of it.

What Happens to Emotions If Collage

Today is not July 26, 1972 but we are with it
presently — where "Time is thin around the cause
and dense around the effect," where On Kawara quotes
the Russian astrophysicist Nikolai Kozyrev,
when today is Dec. 28, 2011 and we forget present, and past,
and persist only in July 26, 1972.

This occurs on Dec 28, 2011.
This occurs in July 26, 1972.

This in January —

A period of intense and demanding work begins with the letter
J in an elongated, white, Gill Sans. If a painting is not finished by
the end of the day, he destroys it.

Or a period of intense and demanding work begins, and is interrupted
by oneself: "Now I have arrived at a brilliant means of articulation
in the field of reproducing nature," Kurt Schwitters writes to Helma
Schwitters. "You see, it is another that paints – I am not he."

On Oct 8, 1983, while Schwitters is living as a refugee in
London, the first Merzbau is destroyed by a bomb, in an air raid
over Hannover, Germany.

On Dec 16, 1951, a second Merzbau, constructed from scratch,
in Lysaker, Oslo, is completely consumed by fire.

While Schwitters does not refer to the cottage in Hjertoya as a
Merzbau, it too is destroyed from neglect and by extreme weather
conditions.

On Kawara destroys a painting of Nov.30.197

On Kawara destroys a painting of 30 Nov 198

In August of 1947, Kurt Schwitters begins work on a third Merzbau, which is left unfinished, and significantly damaged after his death.

"It was my prayer for the victorious end to the war, for once more peace emerged victorious again," Kurt writes to Helma.

Dear Jean,

In attempting to erase an object's original reference, its eigengift, Kurt Schwitters breaks things that are not broken, and fixes things that are, then glues and nails them together, and are Merz.

What happens to emotions if collage propels our chance meeting? Dear, Darling, We find us echoed in a letter.

Dear Jean, I write to you and illegibly in this pastoral are two persons.

Where we find a limit in the thinking of space-time as a reality, or as an abstraction.

On July 4, 1968, On Kawara sees Jovita Perez Franco, Luis Nishizawa, Adela Miazga;

Magdalena Hashimoto, Luis Urias, Alfred Frederic Wyttenbach, also on July 4, 1968.

Dear Jean, I write to you and illegibly, we are two pastorals in this person. Persons are refrains.

We know this from On Kawara's "I Met" where he lists, every day, the names of people he meets from 1968 to 1979.

In a letter to Josef Albers, Helma Schwitters writes: "I do not know whether you know we are no longer allowed to exhibit abstract things here; nor can we show them to anyone, for you don't know if your closest friend will betray you or not."

In "I Met," the presence of Hiroko Hiraoka appears on many days. Helma visits Kurt in Oslo, on June 2, 1939, and this is the last time they meet.

After years of demanding work building the Cathedral of Erotic Misery, Schwitters turns to his friends. "The Big E is finished. All that remains are details in a few places and for that I need material and this is why I am turning to you."

In Kawara, a coherent, narrative, unfolding of a life is made legible through the friends he writes to or meets. A friend receives a postcard that says "I got up " or "I am still alive"

Such that one feels a limit in representations of space-time when thinking of Schwitters and Kawara, and one finds this limit in another person.

In Hiroko Hiraoka and Helma Schwitters.

What is missing in Wilhelm Redemann's photographs of a Merzbau, which is the basis for the reconstructions by Peter Bisseger, is conversation among friends.

In some paradoxes, the limit is when friendship happens. Such that friendship is radiating space.

For Years We Pursue It like Prayer

And I imagine colors too in conversations

leading to the ending,

foaming their phosphorescent streaks.

This hour to the ending is broken.

You take an interest in the dislocation of paths,

while those among us who feel themselves a cipher

undefers the time,

unfolds, at hand, the task,

recites the fragments that be

or may not be our life.

Notes

Each section of "The True Picture of the Past Whizzes By" contains a sentence taken from a corresponding section of Walter Benjamin's On the Concept of History (also Theses on the Philosophy of History) – specifically, the English language version which appears in Vol 4 of "Walter Benjamin: Selected Writings" edited by Michael Jennings from Harvard University Press.

The 15 sections of the serial poem "Work" correspond to the 15 sections of Walter Benjamin's "The Work of Art in the Age of Mechanical Reproduction." Each section of the serial poem is an erasure of a homophonic translation of Benjamin's "Das Kunstwerk im Zeitalter seiner technischen Reproduzierbarkeit." The homophonic translation was carried out using a speech-to-text application.

Acknowledgements

Grateful acknowledgement is made to the editors and staff of publications where versions of these poems appeared:

Apartment Poetry: *"A Fold," "Excursus To Utopia"*

Big Other: *"The True Picture of the Past Whizzes By"*

Black Sun Lit: *"Clothe," "The Given is What Accident Refracts to A Gift," "We Have Altered The Ways In Which We Hear Music," "For Years We Pursue It Like Prayer"*

The Cambridge Literary Review: *"Work"*

The Capilano Review: *"In The Now, You Are Faintly Beginning," "A Dream Of Anechoic Chambers"*

Dreginald: *"The Emergences, The Pause," "Then We Dream You Together," "We Write A Song For The Brandnew Equipment," "What Of Our Renewed Interest In Utopia," "Where What We Feel And The Afternoon Are Topologically The Same"*

Heavy Feather Review: *"What Happens To Emotions If Collage"*

Omniverse: *"Kafkaesque," "Orphic Data Lakes"*

Posit: *"After Music," "What Felt Like the Onset Of An Historical Emotion," "We Requested For Some Relaxing Forest Sounds"*

The White Review: *"So Facture Is The Material Fact Of Joy," "Between The Making Of This Move And This Move," "A House Collaged With Pitch Class Space"*

Lay out your unrest